The Best Part of me

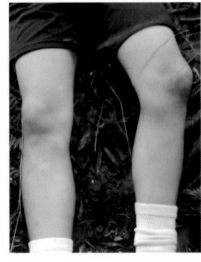

Children talk about their bodies in pictures and words

By Miss Lord's 3, 4, 5th grade class

Photographs by Wendy Ewald

Megan Tingley Books

LITTLE, BROWN AND COMPANY

New York   Boston

FOR LISA LORD AND HER STUDENTS

I would like to thank the Durham, North Carolina, Public Schools and the Center for Documentary Studies for supporting my work as an artist and teacher. In particular I want to acknowledge the teachers and administrators who have participated in the Literacy Through Photography program, beginning with my inspiring collaborator, Lisa Lord. Others who have worked with us are: Denise Friesen, Andrea Bittle, Carolyn Ridout, Robert Hunter, Julia Fairley, Katja Van Brabant-Stevens, Felicia Barnack, Ursula Howard, Audrey Boykin, Cathy Fine, Linda Dimmick, Bryan Woolard, Linda Strickland, Wanda Grantham, Diane Gore, Belinda Sligh, Dietra Arrington, Bill Wirth, Barbi Bailey-Smith, Sophia Faison, Anne Bruton, Cassie Rodriguez, Queen Bass, Brian Fricks, Denise McIntosh Vanessa Calhoun, Terry Simpson, Linda Summerlin, Tamela Davis, Jill Strouhl, Melanie Middleton,Helen Davidson, Emelia DeCroix, and Ada Setzer. As always I must thank my coconspirators over the years — Alan Teasley, Iris Tillman Hill, and Alex Lightfoot, as well as the Literacy Through Photography staff — Dwayne Dixon, Julia Haggson, and Katie Hyde.

Some of the photographs and text in *The Best Part of Me* first appeared in *Double Take* magazine. I am grateful to Robert Coles for seeing its potential, to Alice George and Molly Renda for helping to shape it, to my editor Megan Tingley for seeing it as a book, and to Pete Mauney for making the wonderful prints.

OTHER BOOKS BY WENDY EWALD:

Secret Games: Wendy Ewald Collaborative Works with Children 1969–99, Scalo, 2000
I Wanna Take Me a Picture: Teaching Photography and Writing to Children, Beacon Press, 2001
I Dreamed I Had a Girl in My Pocket, W.W.Norton, 1996
Magic Eyes: Scenes from an Andean Girlhood, Bay Press 1992
Portraits and Dreams: Photographs and Stories by Children of the Appalachians, Writers and Readers, 1985

A portion of the proceeds from *The Best Part of Me* will be donated to
Literacy Through Photography. (www-cds.aas.duke.edu/ltp)

Little, Brown and Company

Hachette Book Group
1290 Avenue of the Americas, New York, NY 10104
Visit our website at www.lb-kids.com

Little, Brown and Company is a division of Hachette Book Group, Inc.
The Little, Brown name and logo are trademarks of Hachette Book Group, Inc.

The publisher is not responsible for websites (or their content) that are not owned by the publisher.

First Edition: January 2002

Library of Congress Cataloging-in-Publication Data

The best part of me : children talk about their bodies in pictures and words / [illustrated] by Wendy Ewald. — 1st ed.
  p.   cm.
  ISBN 978-0-316-70306-2
  1. Children's writings, American.   2. Body, Human — Juvenile poetry.   3. Body, Human —
Pictorial works.   4. Children's poetry, American. [1. Body, Human — Poetry.   2. American poetry.
3. Children's writings.]   I. Ewald, Wendy, ill.   II. Title.
PS 591.S3 B44   2001
810.8'035 — dc21   00-044404

20 19 18

APS
Printed in China

THE BEST PART OF ME is one of several projects I developed in collaboration with teachers and students in the Durham, North Carolina, Public Schools. The work was part of Literacy Through Photography, a program I originated at the Center for Documentary Studies at Duke University to use photography as a starting point for writing.

Over the past few years, photography has gotten more and more interested in the human body and in issues that arise when portraying children. I became curious about how the children regarded their bodies. In working as an artist and a teacher, I often ask people to create self-portraits in writing or photographs. Many times I've heard children describe themselves and their kinships with others in terms of parts of their bodies — "I have Mom's eyes," one of my students from Kentucky told me. "They're real little."

I asked second- through fifth-grade students at Club Boulevard Elementary School to choose the parts of their bodies they liked best or that explained the most about them. Then, using a view camera so I could focus as closely as I needed, I took a Polaroid picture of each child. The child and I then looked at the photograph together and discussed changes in composition or background that might reflect the child's vision of him- or herself. Once we were satisfied with the image, the child took it back into the classroom and worked with Lisa Lord, an extraordinarily gifted writing teacher.

Once we decided to make a book of the photographs and writings, I asked the students to help me design and title it. Beverly Benton chose her back and her hair, and likened herself to a Barbie doll. Tim McKoy asked me to photograph his chest because he depended on it, he said, to protect himself. Although Tramika Davis and Colette Cosner both chose their hands, they described them differently. Tramika's description alluded to the work they'd done, Colette's to the graceful protection and magic her hands brought her.

When I looked at the assembled pictures and text, I was startled by how revealing they were about the individual students and about how the different cultural groups conceived of their bodies and thought about them. It's my hope that this book will give children a chance to talk about their bodies and share their candid sense of themselves with adults, for whom intimacy and familiarity — what is plainly visible — are often at odds.

My eyes are brown and black.
Big and round.
I see lots of colors around.
I see me I see you.
I like my eyes I should not be
surprised. I see your eyes I see my eyes.
I know my eyes can see within me.
without eyes you couldn't see not one
tree you couldn't see.
Not one eye you couldn't buy.

The eye is good the eye is mad when
you are mad it can seem very

sad.

Denyea Elliott

I like my feet because
I painted the toe nails
and because I cut them
not too short and not too
long!

Mosquitoes like my legs
(Blood) I take after my
Dad because they like
his blood. I have
long legs. I picked to
put my feet on leaves
because I like to play
and I couldn't run and
play without them.

Signature : Martha
Benton

✫ My hair ✫

I like my hair its long, black and wavy. If you look real close you can see red streaks. It comes from my mexican heritage. Its wavy like the ocean

✫ By: Camila Villasana ✫

I need my arms to pick up my little brothers and throw them on the bed but when they get up and they try to kick me in my head when I'm sleeping in the bed.

But they can't as long as I have my arms over my head.

Chris Ice mitchell

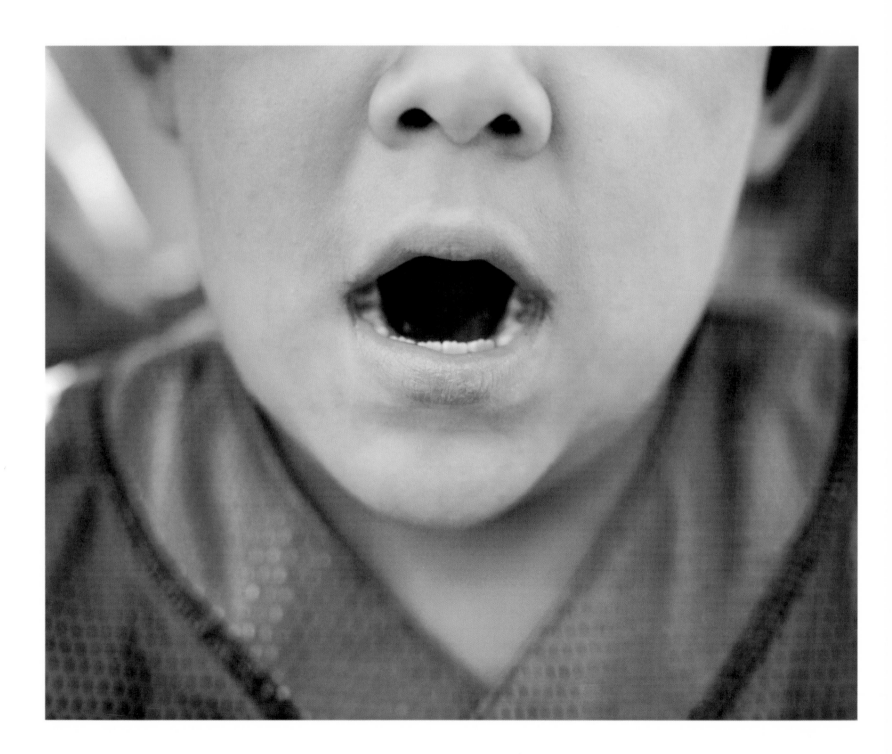

Some times I can move my teeth.
some times my granma can move her
teeth too. Did You Know baby teeth
are smoother then permanent teeth?
I can bite and eat with my teeth
I have sharp teeth. so does a shark and my
cousin laura.

Alejandro Espinosa

My Hands

I like my hands because they turn the pages of a book slowly and magically. Reading makes me happy. They wipe my eyes when I am sad. They threaten the things that make me mad. They pull the covers over my head when I am scared. They feel my forehead when I am sick. They write what I am writing now. They touch the precious earth and ground. They dance. They act. They're slender and unige. They're mine— thats all, slender and unique.

Colette Cosner

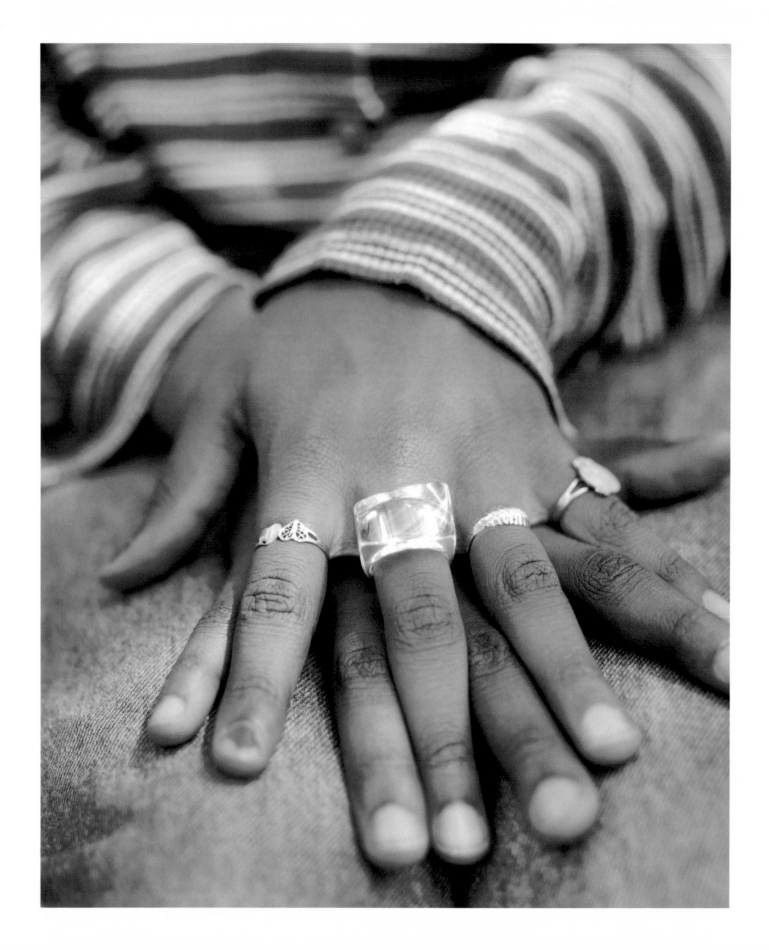

My Hands

By: Tramika Davis

Ohhh. My hands. My old wrinkled hands. Can't you see the triangles in both of them? In the picture I have on 2 real rings, 1 plastic ring, and 1 fake tweety bird ring. I have no ring on my thumb. My hands are big, I say strong. I lift some -things that are heavy. Maybe thats why they're big and ugly. The reason why my nails are'nt long is, because I bite them off.

I write with my right hand but if write with my left it looks sloppy. See the reason why I choose my hands is becau- -se I like them even if they're big and ugly.

My Elbow

My elbow is like a little circle. I'm using my elbow when I'm mad. I put my hand on my waist and my elbow sticks out. My elbows are on a table when I'm writing or reading. I like my elbows because I play with my elbows when I jump rope.

By: Mari Garcia

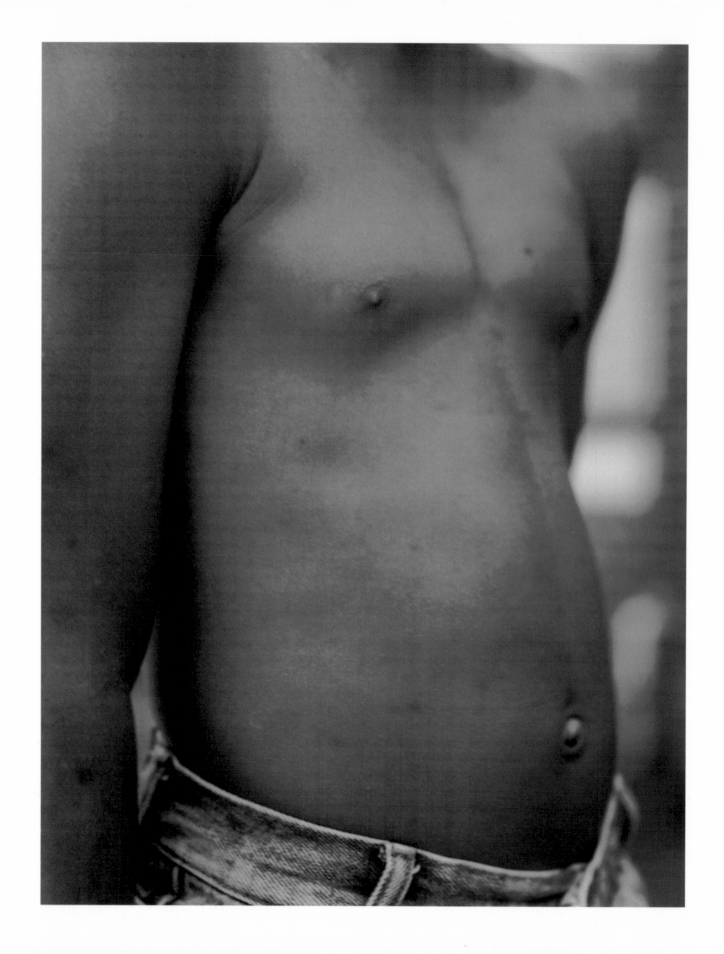

Tim McKoy

Chest, Chest you're the best.
I like to rest on you, oh yes.
I wake up. I depend on you
to protect my body too.
  Chest, Chest, you're the best
you're a big success you might
be the best in the west.
  Chest, Chest, you're the best.

The Knee Poem

A scar - the scar is a circle!

Some designs like lines and stripes!
long legs!

Summer time - taken in the summer time!
Background is the grass!
Hard legs - legs are hard!
my sweater's under my legs!
I can jump good with these knees!
(These knees are Hispanic!)

Laura Molina

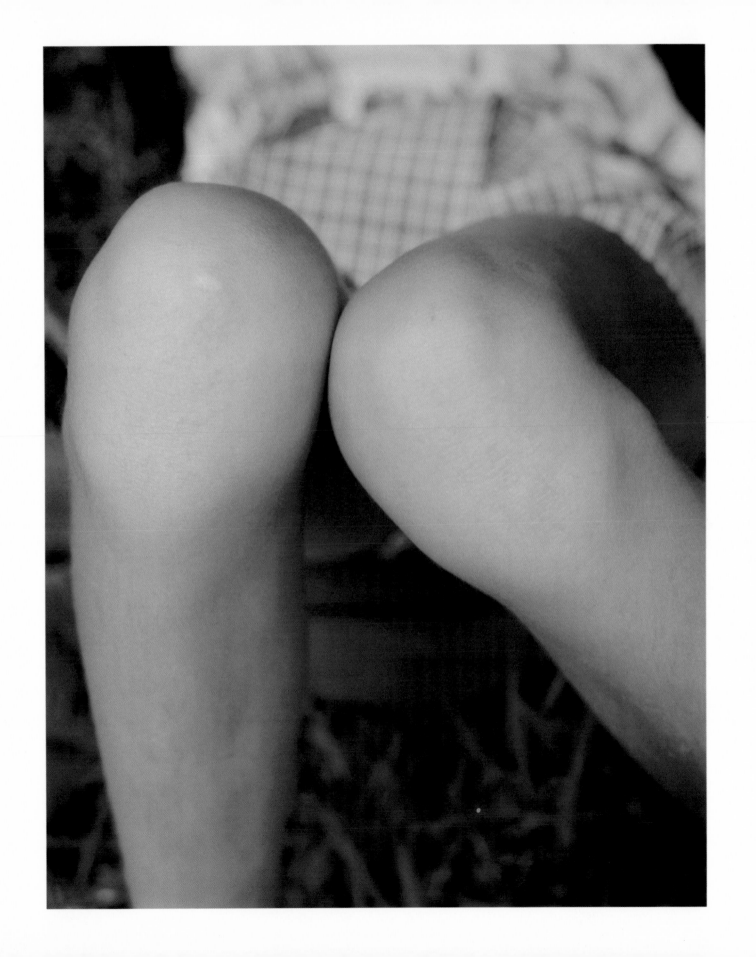

Matthew
Culbreth

The reason I took a picture
of my face is because my
mom says that I look like her
because my mom thinks that I
have nice eyes. Sometimes I like to
squint my eyes when I am in the
sun. My eyes are light blue as
my mom's are blue to. My hair is
the same as my moms, dads and my
brothers.

My back

I picked my back because if
I did'nt have my back then I
couldn't move because every thing
counts on my back.
And I put hair in the picture
because I like my hair.
I can put barrets in my hair
and I can braid it. My mom
braids my hair a lot. she
Says I am her little Barbie.
My hair is longer than my short
Sleeve shirt.

By: Beverly Benton

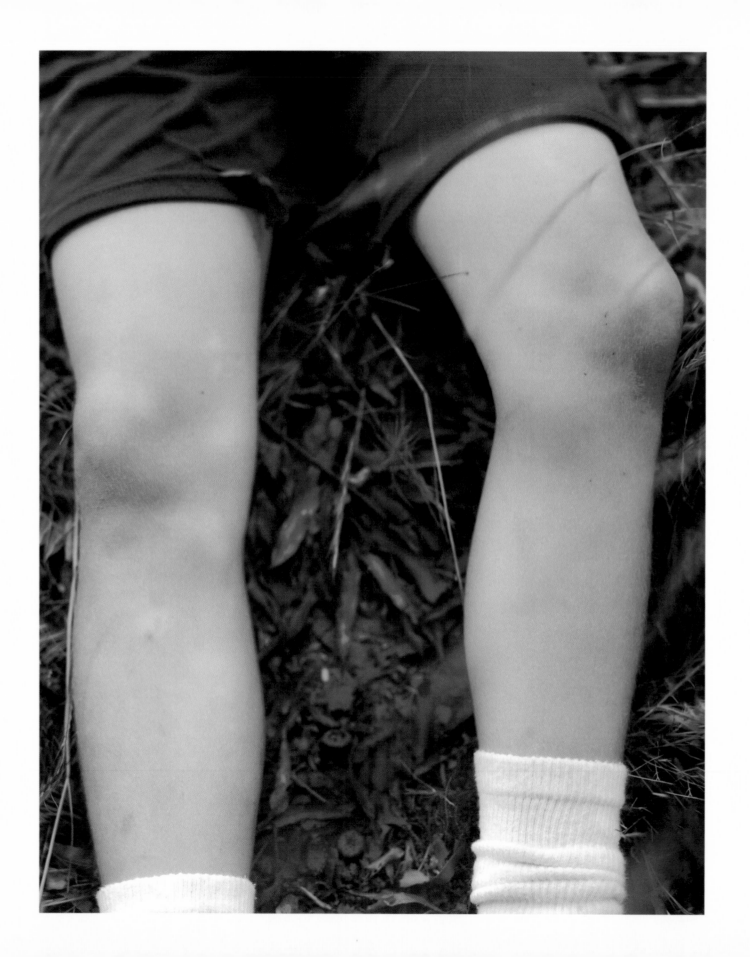

MY WONDERFUL LEGS!

By Andrew Legge

Legs, Legs, you carry me a long way,
You hold me up when I'm out to play.
Legs, Legs, you're so strong,
So that I'm able to run very long.
You get very tired when I rollerblade
But you still go on,
That's how strong you are made.
You don't get hurt very easily,
I just hate when people call
you measly.

My Neck!

I Love my neck,
My Neck holds the beautiful
necklaces that I wear.
I Love my Neck because
it is not too big or not
too small. It is Just right
for me. I love my neck
for all the things it can
do. It connects to my
Lovely Face and to my
strong body. It holds my
head. I Like my neck. That
is why it is the Best Part of me!

By: Lidia Johnson

All Mine ☯

When I pray my hands
over lap

In the sun they shine

The color of my hands
is toasty brown

These beautiful things
are mine.

By: Nada Hussain